discover countries

The EU Countries

Rob Bowden

WAYLAND

First published in paperback in 2012

Wayland
Hachette Children's Books
338 Euston Road
London NW1 3BH

Wayland Australia
Level 17/207 Kent Street,
Sydney, NSW 2000

Concept design: Jason Billin
Editor: Kelly Davis
Designer: Amy Sparks
Picture research: Amy Sparks
All maps: Stefan Chabluk
Consultant: Elaine Jackson

Produced for Wayland by
White-Thomson Publishing Ltd

www.wtpub.co.uk
+44 (0)843 2087 460

British Library Cataloguing in Publication Data
Rob Bowden, 1973-
The EU Countries -- (Discover countries)
1. European Union countries--Juvenile literature
I. Title II. Series   341.2'422-dc22
ISBN: 978 07502 7087 8
Printed in China

Wayland is a division of Hachette Children's Books
an Hachette UK company
www.hachette.co.uk
First published in 2011 by Wayland

All data in this book was updated in 2012
and has been collected from the latest sources available at that time.

Picture credits
1 & 18, Shutterstock/Yarygin; 3 (top) & 6, Shutterstock/Andrea Seemann; 3 (bottom) & 27, Shutterstock/alysta; 5, Shutterstock/Philiphalle; 7, Shutterstock/Graça Victoria; 8, Dreamstime/Felinda; 9, Shutterstock/Tobias Machhaus; 10, Shutterstock/PHB.cz (Richard Semik); 11, Shutterstock/Canoneer; 12, Shutterstock/ollirg; 13, Shutterstock/Freddy Eliasson; 14, Shutterstock/bofotolux; 15, Shutterstock/interlight; 16, Shutterstock/Yory Frenklakh; 17, Dreamstime/Fotokate; 19, Shutterstock/Rodion; 20, Shutterstock/walshphotos; 21, Shutterstock/Darren Pierse Kelly; 22, Shutterstock/David Hughes; 23, Shutterstock/Alex Yeung; 24, Shutterstock/Maugli; 25, Shutterstock/David H. Seymour; 26, Shutterstock/Marta P; 28, Shutterstock/Christopher Elwell; 29, Dreamstime/Vanbeets; 30, Shutterstock/Tupungato; 31, Dreamstime/Videowok; 32, Shutterstock/ Oleksiy Mark; 33, Shutterstock/Palis Michalis; 34, Shutterstock/S. Borisov; 35, Shutterstock/Aleksei Volkov; 36, Shutterstock/Biczó Zsolt; 37, Shutterstock/Vladimirs Koskins; 38, Shutterstock/Shmel; 39, Shutterstock/Cecilia Lim H M; 40, Shutterstock/puchan; 41, Shutterstock/PHB.cz (Richard Semik); 42, Shutterstock/Simon Krzic; 43, Shutterstock/melki76; 44, Shutterstock/Boerescu; 45, istockphoto/Davor Lovincic; cover (right) Shutterstock/Skowron; cover (left) Dreamstime/Milonk.

Contents

What is the EU?

A history of the EU

The origins of the European Union (EU) can be traced to the years following World War II when European nations started looking for ways to expand their economies peacefully and co-operatively. Originally, in 1951, just six countries (Belgium, Germany, France, Italy, Luxembourg and the Netherlands) signed an agreement to co-operate over trade in steel and coal. By 1957 this agreement had been widened to include other trade and became the European Economic Community (EEC). The UK, Ireland and Denmark joined the EEC in 1973, followed by three more nations in the 1980s (Greece in 1981, and Spain and Portugal in 1986).

The EU today

In the 1970s and 1980s the EEC began to take on non-economic roles such as creating rules that applied to the whole of Europe. These included measures to protect the environment, human rights and justice. A development fund also helped poorer nations to build infrastructure. In 1992 a new agreement created the European Union as it is today. This agreement included plans for a single European currency, the euro, introduced in 1999. Three years later, in 2002, the euro replaced national notes and coins in 12 of the 15 EU nations (Austria, Finland and Sweden had joined in 1995).

Facts at a glance

Year EU was founded: 1951

Members: 27

Total area: 4,324,782 sq km (1,669,807 sq miles)

Climate:
Cool temperate; potentially subarctic in the north to temperate; mild wet winters; hot dry summers in the south

Highest point: Mont Blanc, France 4,807 m (15,771 ft)

Lowest points:
Lammefjord, Denmark -7 m (-23 ft)
Zuidplaspolder, Netherlands -7 m (-23 ft)

Population: 499,400,000

Largest cities:
Paris 10,485,000
London 8,615,000
Barcelona 5,851,000
Madrid 5,083,000
Berlin 3,450,000
Rome 3,362,000

Capital cities of EU:
Brussels (Belgium), Strasbourg (France), Luxembourg

Life expectancy at birth:
Male 76 years;
Female 82 years

Official languages: Bulgarian, Czech, Danish, Dutch, English, Estonian, Finnish, French, Gaelic, German, Greek, Hungarian, Italian, Latvian, Lithuanian, Maltese, Polish, Portuguese, Romanian, Slovak, Slovene, Spanish, Swedish

Currency: 1 euro = 100 cents

GDP:
US$14.4 trillion; per capita US$32,500

Natural resources:
Iron ore, natural gas, petroleum, coal, copper, lead, zinc, bauxite, uranium, potash, salt, hydroelectric power, arable land, timber, fish

The EU now has 27 member nations, with ten joining in 2004 (mainly from Eastern Europe) and two more joining in 2007. Together they form one of the world's largest and most powerful organisations. The EU is likely to grow further still as more nations seek to join and benefit from membership.

EU in the world

The countries of the EU include most of the European continent. Its combined population of almost half a billion is larger than that of the USA and four times greater than Japan's. The economies of the EU make up around 22 per cent of world economic production (compared to 20.5 per cent for the USA and 6.5 per cent for Japan). The strength of the EU is largely due to the trading freedom it allows between member nations. In addition, individuals can travel between EU countries with minimal barriers. Many people living in EU countries, for example, find work in other EU nations. The introduction of the euro, now used by 17 EU members, has further helped trade.

The nations of the EU are major contributors to world culture and have produced many famous writers, thinkers, musicians and artists. They have also pioneered scientific and technological advances, from the first factories in the eighteenth century, through to the invention of the World Wide Web and the exploration of space. Although EU nations share an increasing amount, each still has its own character and particular features, whether it be dramatic landscapes, national customs or speciality foods. This book will introduce you to the geography, society, economy and culture of the countries that make up the European Union.

The flags of the member nations and the flag of the EU fly outside the European Parliament building in Strasbourg, France. The European Parliament also has premises in Brussels and Luxembourg.

DID YOU KNOW?

The European Union is less than half the size of the United States, but its population is over 50 per cent larger.

Belgium

Belgium occupies an important geographical and political location between France and Germany. It was a founder member of the EU and its capital, Brussels, is home to the European Parliament and the Council of the European Union.

Geography

Much of Belgium is flat and low-lying, with a coastal plain extending into the country from the North Sea and the Netherlands. This region is known as Flanders and includes polders (land that has been reclaimed from the sea and is protected by dunes and dykes). The region is criss-crossed with many canals. The centre of Belgium is a fertile farming region, with many small

Facts at a glance

Year of EU entry: 1951

Land area: 30,278 sq km (11,690 sq miles)

Climate:
Temperate; mild winters; cool summers; rainy; humid; cloudy

Highest point:
Mount Botrange 694 m (2,277 ft)

Lowest point:
North Sea 0 m (0 ft)

Political system:
Constitutional monarchy

Population: 10.8 million

Urban population: 97%

Largest cities:
Brussels (capital) 1,904,000
Antwerp 965,000

Life expectancy at birth:
Male 76 years;
Female 83 years

Official languages:
Dutch, French, German

Ethnic composition:
Fleming 58%, Walloon 31%, mixed or other 11%

Religious affiliation:
Roman Catholic 75%, other (includes Protestant) 25%

Currency:
1 euro = 100 cents

GDP:
US$383.4 billion, per capita US$36,800

Natural resources:
Construction materials, silica sand, carbonates

▼ Bruges, in the Flanders region of Belgium, is a historic town known for its canals and its chocolate. It is a popular tourist destination.

BELGIUM

tributaries feeding into Belgium's longest river, the Schelde (also Scheldt). In the south-east of Belgium, the Ardennes region is more hilly and forested. It includes Mount Botrange – Belgium's highest point.

The coastal lowlands are the warmest and driest region, while the Ardennes is wetter and cooler, with regular winter frosts and around 30 days of snow per year. Brussels, in the centre of the country, has an average low of around 0°C (32°F) in January and an average high of 22°C (71°F) in July.

Society

Belgium is socially split between Dutch-speaking Flanders in the north and French-speaking Wallonia in the south. Located between these two areas is the bilingual capital, Brussels, where both Dutch and French share official language status. There are considerable divisions between Flanders and Wallonia and the government is therefore normally a coalition, including representatives of both regions.

Economy and industry

As Belgium is a small country with relatively few natural resources, it has instead developed its economy very successfully by processing imported raw materials and exporting the resulting products. Its reserves of coal helped Belgium to develop a major steel industry in the nineteenth century, but as the coal has run out, this industry has declined. Metal processing is still important, along with chemical, textile, glass, paper and food-processing industries. Belgium has several specialised high-value industries, including lace, diamonds and the famous Belgian chocolates. The service sector accounts for around 75 per cent of the economy. Banking, business services, trade and tourism are particularly important and have been greatly boosted by Belgium's role in hosting the EU headquarters in Brussels.

Brussels, in the heart of Belgium, hosts the main headquarters of the EU. The city is famous for its modern architecture, including the Atomium Sculpture in Heysel Park.

Belgian culture

Belgium is famous for its architecture and Flemish art dating from the fifteenth to the seventeenth centuries. Famous painters from this period include Pieter Bruegel the Elder and Peter Paul Rubens. Food and beer are another important part of the culture, and the Belgians claim to have invented French fries. Some of Belgium's best-known cultural exports are its comic strips. The most famous of these is *Tintin*, about an adventurous boy and his friends, which was created by Hergé (the pen name of Georges Remi) in 1929.

Germany

Germany is the wealthiest and most populated country in the EU. It has a turbulent history of war and division but, as a founding member of the EU, Germany has also been at the forefront of building a modern and peaceful Europe.

Geography

Germany is bordered by nine European countries and by the North Sea and Baltic Sea to the north. Northern Germany is a lowland area. The country then gradually slopes upwards through the central German uplands and into the Bavarian Alps in the far south, where Zugspitze (the country's highest point) is found. Germany has several large rivers, including the Danube and Elbe, but the longest is the Rhine.

Facts at a glance

Year of EU entry: 1951

Land area: 348,672 sq km (134,622 sq miles)

Climate: Temperate; marine

Highest point: Zugspitze 2,963 m (9,721 ft)

Lowest point: Neuendorf bei Wilster -3.54 m (-11.6 ft)

Population: 82.1 million

Urban population: 74%

Largest cities:
Berlin (capital) 3,450,000
Hamburg 1,786,000
Munich 1,349,000
Cologne 1,001,000

Life expectancy at birth:
Male 76 years;
Female 83 years

Political system: Federal republic

Official language: German

Ethnic composition: German 91.5%, Turkish 2.4%, other 6.1% (made up largely of Greek, Italian, Polish, Russian, Serbo-Croatian, Spanish)

Religious affiliation: Protestant 34%, Roman Catholic 34%, Muslim 3.7%, unaffiliated or other 28.3%

Currency: 1 euro = 100 cents

GDP: US$2.81 trillion; per capita US$34,100

Natural resources: Coal, lignite, natural gas, iron ore, copper, nickel, uranium, potash, salt, construction materials, timber, arable land

◀ Famous for its dramatic scenery, the Rhine is an important transport route for industry and the busiest inland waterway in Europe.

Germany has a generally mild climate that becomes wetter and cooler as you move south into the highlands. Although warmer for much of the year, Germany's northern plain is often the coldest part of the country in the winter because it gets winds from Scandinavia.

Society

Until 1990, Germany was divided between West and East Germany. West Germany was more powerful and wealthier, and a founder member of the EU. East Germany, by contrast, had close ties with the former USSR (now Russia) and was much poorer. Since reunification, many people have moved from the East into the West in the hope of finding better jobs and an improved quality of life. The new unified government has spent billions of euros on improving eastern regions, but there are still major social divisions. Unemployment in some eastern areas is over 20 per cent, compared to around 7.5 per cent nationally.

Economy and industry

Germany has the biggest economy in the EU and one of the largest in the world. It is a major engineering, chemical and manufacturing nation, known for its highly skilled workers and advanced technology. With a large export sector, many German companies – including Siemens, BMW and Mercedes – have become world-famous brands. Services make up around 70 per cent of the economy and include banking and finance centred in Frankfurt, the location of the European Central Bank.

⬧ After reunification, Berlin once again became the capital of Germany. It has been transformed by new buildings such as these government offices along the River Spree.

German culture

Great German writers and thinkers include Johann Wolfgang von Goethe, Immanuel Kant and Friedrich Wilhelm Nietzsche. Germany has also produced world-famous classical composers such as Johann Sebastian Bach, Ludwig van Beethoven, Johannes Brahms and Richard Wagner. Germany is well known for its hearty food, including many different types of sausage (*Wurst*). The annual Oktoberfest in Munich is a celebration of German food and beer, which attracts over six million visitors.

France

France is the largest country in the EU, at a little over twice the area of the UK. It is also one of the most influential nations in the EU, from its role as a founding member to its part in discussions about the EU's future.

Geography

France is roughly hexagon-shaped, with coasts along the English Channel to the north, the Atlantic Ocean to the west and the Mediterranean Sea in the south. It has borders with Spain and Andorra in the southwest, and Italy, Switzerland, Germany, Belgium and Luxembourg to the east. Most of France is made up of low-lying plains and plateaux, with large upland areas called massifs. The Massif Central covers about a sixth of France and is the source of France's longest river, the Loire, which flows 1,020 km (634 miles) to the Atlantic Ocean.

Facts at a glance

Year of EU entry: 1951

Land area: 549,970 sq km (212,345 sq miles)

Climate: Variable (see page 11)

Highest point: Mont Blanc 4,807 m (15,771 ft)

Lowest point: Rhone river delta -2 m (-7 ft)

Political system: Republic

Population: 64.3 million

Urban population: 85%

Largest cities:
Paris (capital) 10,485,000
Marseilles 1,469,000
Lyon 1,468,000

Life expectancy at birth:
Male 78 years;
Female 84 years

Official language:
French

Ethnic composition:
Celtic and Latin with Teutonic, Slavic, North African, Indochinese, Basque minorities

Religious affiliation:
Roman Catholic 83%–88%, Protestant 2%, Jewish 1%, Muslim 5%–10%, unaffiliated 4%

Currency:
1 euro = 100 cents

GDP:
US$2.11 trillion; per capita US$32,600

Natural resources:
Coal, iron ore, bauxite, zinc, uranium, antimony, arsenic, potash, feldspar, fluorspar, gypsum, timber, fish

The Millau Viaduct, in southern France, is one of the highest and longest road bridges in the world. It is a modern symbol of France's proud engineering and design industries.

The Alps along France's eastern border include the highest mountain in France and the EU, Mont Blanc. Another mountain chain, the Pyrenees, forms the border with Spain and Andorra.

France's climate varies from mild and temperate in the north to a warmer and drier Mediterranean climate in the south. Across the country, highland regions are cooler and have higher precipitation. The Alps and the Pyrenees have long periods under snowfall, making them popular winter sport destinations.

Society

France has a diverse society that reflects its history of exploration, empire and migration. It has many people originating from North Africa, for example – a region that was once under French control. The French are often said to be very nationalistic, and especially protective of their language and culture.

Economy and industry

France has one of the strongest economies in the EU. Electronics, chemicals, fashion, information technology and car production are among its most important industries. Aerospace technology is also important and France is a lead nation in Airbus, the company that produces many of the world's passenger aircraft. France is a world leader in engineering, having completed famous projects including the Channel Tunnel linking France to the UK and the spectacular Millau Viaduct in southern France (see page 10). Agriculture remains an important sector and French produce, particularly wine and cheese, is highly valued around the world. Service industries, such as banking, telecoms and insurance, account for most of France's income. Tourism is especially important and France receives around 75 million visitors per year, more than any other country in the world.

The famous Eiffel Tower, above the River Seine in Paris, is a big attraction for the millions of tourists who visit France every year.

French culture

Many of Europe's most famous artists, including Renoir, Monet, Cezanne, Gauguin and Matisse, have been French. The country is also known for writers and thinkers such as Descartes, Pascal, Rousseau, Flaubert and Sartre. France continues to push the frontiers of art and culture, with a reputation for daring designs in architecture, fashion and cars, for example. In 2010, UNESCO listed French cuisine as a vital part of the world's cultural heritage.

Italy

Italy was the only southern European nation to be a founding member of the EU and it has maintained a central role in the EU ever since. The Italian mainland also contains two small independent states, Vatican City (in Rome) and San Marino.

Geography

Italy juts out from the European mainland into the Mediterranean Sea in a boot shape, with the island of Sicily at its toe. The island of Sardinia to the west is also part of Italy, together with around 70 smaller islands. Most of Italy is mountainous, with the Alps acting as the northern border and the Apennines stretching southwards down the length of the country. Plains in the north form the main lowland region and surround Italy's largest river, the Po, which flows for 652 km (405 miles) to the Adriatic Sea.

⬥ Mount Etna, one of the most active volcanoes in the EU, looms over the Sicilian countryside.

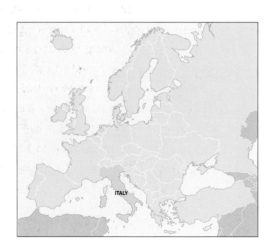

Facts at a glance

Year of EU entry: 1951

Land area: 294,140 sq km (113,568 sq miles)

Climate: Predominantly Mediterranean; Alpine in far north; hot, dry in south

Highest point: Mont Blanc de Courmayeur 4,748 m (15,577 ft)

Lowest point: Mediterranean Sea 0 m (0 ft)

Political system: Republic

Population: 60 million

Urban population: 68%

Largest cities:
Rome (capital) 3,362,000
Milan 2,967,000
Naples 2,292,000

Life expectancy at birth:
Male 77 years;
Female 83 years

Official languages:
Italian

Ethnic composition:
Italian (includes German-, French-, and Slovene-Italians in the north and Albanian-Italians and Greek-Italians in the south)

Religious affiliation:
Roman Catholic 90%, other 10% (Protestant, Jewish, Muslim)

Currency: 1 euro = 100 cents

GDP:
US$1.74 trillion; per capita US$29,900

Natural resources:
Coal, mercury, zinc, potash, marble, barite, asbestos, pumice, fluorspar, feldspar, pyrite (sulphur), natural gas and crude oil reserves, fish, arable land

Southern Italy is a volcanic region and includes four active volcanoes. Mount Vesuvius, outside Naples, last erupted in 1944, but is more famous for the eruption of 79 CE that buried the Roman city of Pompeii in ash. The excavated ruins of Pompeii are now a major tourist attraction. Mount Etna, on the island of Sicily, is highly active and erupts regularly. The neighbouring island of Stromboli is also a highly active volcano, sometimes called 'the lighthouse of the Mediterranean' because of its regular shows of red-hot lava.

 The ruins of the Forum, the heart of ancient Rome, contrast with the sprawling modern city of Rome behind.

Society

A history of conquest and invasion means that many Italians can trace their ethnic origins back to people from Greece, Albania, Germany, France and other countries. This ethnic mixing continues today with recent immigration to Italy from North Africa, Latin America, South-East Asia and Eastern Europe. Immigration is important to Italy because falling birth rates and an ageing population have left the economy short of workers.

Economy and industry

Italy is among the strongest economies in the EU. Its industries include metals and engineering, manufacturing, electronics, car production, textiles, fashion, tourism and food processing. The northern regions dominate the economy, producing most of Italy's wealth and counting as one of the richest regions in the EU. Southern Italy is much poorer and is heavily reliant on agriculture and tourism for its income. High-value crops, such as olives and grapes (for wine), are especially important.

Italian culture

From its fine architecture, to its flare for design, to its love of good food and its history of great artists, Italy is one of the most culturally rich nations in the world. International tourists come to marvel at its buildings, to enjoy its food and to visit galleries containing works by artists such as Botticelli, Leonardo da Vinci, Michelangelo and Caravaggio. Opera is another great Italian art form and Italy boasts both Verdi and Puccini in its list of famous operatic composers. For many people, Italy is best known for its wonderful cuisine and for introducing the world to foods such as pizza, pasta, pesto and risotto.

Luxembourg

Luxembourg is a small country surrounded by France, Germany and Belgium. Its population of just half a million is among the wealthiest in the world. Luxembourg is highly reliant on trade and relationships with EU nations. It is also home to the Court of Justice of the European Union.

Geography

Luxembourg is just 82 km (51 miles) long from north to south and only 56 km (35 miles) wide from east to west. Its northern third is mountainous and forms part of the Ardennes mountain chain with Belgium. It is forested, with steep gorges carved by mountain rivers that feed the River Sûre before it joins the Moselle River on the German border. Southern Luxembourg is made up of gentle hills and open plains.

Facts at a glance

Year of EU entry: 1951

Land area: 2,586 sq km (998 sq miles)

Climate: Modified continental; moderate

Highest point: Buurgplaatz 559 m (1,834 ft)

Lowest point: Moselle River 133 m (436 ft)

Political system: Constitutional monarchy

Population: 0.5 million

Urban population: 82%

Largest city: Luxembourg City (capital) <750,000

Life expectancy at birth: Male 76 years; Female 83 years

Official languages: German, French

Ethnic composition: Luxembourger 63.1%, Portuguese 13.3%, French 4.5%, Italian 4.3%, German 2.3%, other EU 7.3%, other 5.2%

Religious affiliation: Roman Catholic 87%, other (includes Protestant, Jewish, and Muslim) 13%

Currency: 1 euro = 100 cents

GDP: US$39.1 billion; per capita US$79,600

Natural resources: Iron ore (no longer exploited), arable land

Luxembourg is one of the less famous EU wine-producing nations, but the wines of the Moselle region are among the best in Europe.

14

It is on these plains that most people live and where the capital city is located, straddling the Alzette River.

Luxembourg has a mild and wet climate with few extremes. Temperatures in the capital range from around 0.7°C (33°F) in January to 17°C (63°F) in July. The north is generally cooler and wetter and the Moselle valley has a warmer and sunnier climate that is ideal for grape-growing and wine production (see page 14).

Society

Although they are relatively few in number, Luxembourgers are a proud people who have managed to maintain a strong sense of national identity. This includes having their own language called Luxembourgish, though in practice French and German are also widely used as official and popular languages.

Economy and industry

Luxembourg developed its economy using iron ore deposits to make steel. In the 1960s steel made up around 80 per cent of the country's exports, but by the 1980s the iron ore had run out. Luxembourg still has an industrial sector focused on chemicals, metals and rubber, but most of the economy now centres on services such as banking and insurance. Many international companies have their European headquarters in Luxembourg because of its low taxes and good location. Farming in Luxembourg is mainly based on livestock and dairy produce, with some grain and vegetable growing.

One benefit of EU membership is that workers can travel freely to work in other EU nations. This is important to Luxembourg, with foreign or cross-border workers making up around 60 per cent of its labour force.

⬤ Luxembourg City lies in the southern part of the country. It is over 1000 years old and was the European Capital of Culture in 2007.

Luxembourg's culture

Luxembourg's culture draws on the cultures of its surrounding nations, but adds its own flavour from its industrial past and its history as a European crossroads. Its painters, sculptors, orchestras and theatres are not as well known as those of other EU nations, but Luxembourg is very supportive of the arts, with many museums, galleries and other exhibition spaces including a new museum of modern art, the Mudam, which was designed by Ieoh Ming Pei (famous for the glass pyramid at the Louvre in Paris).

The Netherlands

The Netherlands occupies an important location in Europe and acts as a hub for transport and trade between EU nations and the wider world. It has been a key member of the EU since the beginning.

Geography

Over half of the Netherlands lies less than 1 m (3 feet) above sea level and around a quarter is below sea level. This land is vulnerable to flooding from the North Sea to the north and from the rivers that cross the Netherlands. The Dutch have overcome this problem by building a series of dams or dykes to hold the water back and protect the land. Behind these dykes, the land has been drained and reclaimed for use as farmland or for building homes and factories. Known as polders, this artificial land is extremely flat.

Facts at a glance

Year of EU entry: 1951

Land area: 33,893 sq km (13,086 sq miles)

Climate: Temperate; marine

Highest point: Vaalserberg 322 m (1,056 ft)

Lowest point: Zuidplaspolder -7 m (-23 ft)

Political system: Constitutional monarchy

Population: 16.5 million

Urban population: 83%

Largest cities: Amsterdam (capital) 1,049, 000 Rotterdam 1,010,000

Life expectancy at birth: Male 77 years; Female 82 years

Official languages: Dutch, Frisian

Ethnic composition: Dutch 80.7%, EU 5%, Indonesian 2.4%, Turkish 2.2%, Surinamese 2%, Moroccan 2%, Netherlands Antilles & Aruba 0.8%, other 4.8%

Religious affiliation: Roman Catholic 30%, Dutch Reformed 11%, Calvinist 6%, other Protestant 3%, Muslim 5.8%, other 2.2%, none 42%

Currency: 1 euro = 100 cents

GDP: US$660 billion; per capita US$39,500

Natural resources: Natural gas, petroleum, peat, limestone, salt, sand and gravel, arable land

◀ Amsterdam is a city dominated by water, which has always been important for trading. For centuries, people and goods have come to Amsterdam from around the world and made it one of the EU's most diverse cities.

In 1986 three polders were united to create a new province called Flevoland. Several large rivers, including the Rhine, Lek, Waal and Meuse, end their journey to the sea by passing through the Netherlands. The Rhine is especially important, as it handles large volumes of river trade and connects inland Europe with the outside world through Rotterdam – the largest port in Europe.

The Netherlands has a mild climate with regular rainfall throughout the year and cloudy skies for much of the time. It is influenced by warm air (the Gulf Stream) that travels across the Atlantic and prevents winter temperatures becoming too cold.

Society

The Netherlands is famous for having a very welcoming, open society that is tolerant of different religions and ways of life. Its population originates from many different areas of Europe, South America, Asia and Africa and around a fifth of all its people were either born overseas or have a parent who was. The larger cities, such as Amsterdam, Rotterdam, The Hague and Utrecht, are especially multicultural and have a very international atmosphere, with many different types of food and a real mixing of cultures.

Economy and industry

Services such as banking, tourism and trading are the main sources of income for the Netherlands, but manufacturing and agriculture both play an important part too. Manufacturing is focused on food processing, metals, electronics, chemicals and hi-tech industries such as biotechnology and microelectronics. Agriculture is dominated by livestock (especially pigs), dairy farming, and high-value fruit and vegetables, which are mostly grown in glasshouses. The Netherlands is the centre of the global flower industry and the world's largest flower auction in the town of Aalsmeer sells flowers from across the world.

Dutch culture

The Netherlands has produced some of the world's best-known and most influential painters such as Rembrandt and Van Gogh. Local traditions and customs remain strong in the Netherlands and are celebrated through festivals such as the Keukenhof Tulip Festival. The multicultural population has had a big impact on the culture of the Netherlands. One of the most popular foods, for example, is the 'rice table', a way of trying many different dishes in a single meal that was brought to the Netherlands from its colonies in Indonesia.

▼ The Netherlands is famous for its flowers. These tulips are being grown on a large commercial farm.

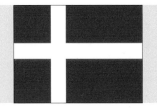

Denmark

Denmark was the first of the Scandinavian countries to join the EU. It enjoys many benefits of being in the EU, but chose not to adopt the euro as its currency. Denmark has a strong economy and a relatively small population (about half that of Paris), with a high standard of living.

Geography

Denmark occupies the Jutland Peninsula, which separates the North Sea and the Baltic Sea. To the east of this peninsula are around 400 islands but only 82 are inhabited. The largest two islands are Funen and Zealand. Most of Denmark lies at less than 30 m (100 feet) above sea level and generally consists of flat plains or gently rolling hills.

○ Brightly coloured buildings line Nyhavn Harbour in the Danish capital Copenhagen. Like many old industrial centres in the EU, Nyhavn has now been redeveloped as a tourist centre.

Facts at a glance

Year of EU entry: 1973

Land area: 42,434 sq km (16,384 sq miles)

Climate: Variable (see page 19)

Highest point: Yding Skovhoej 173 m (568 ft)

Lowest point: Lammefjord -7 m (-23 ft)

Political system: Constitutional monarchy

Population: 5.5 million

Urban population: 87%

Largest city: Copenhagen (capital) 1,186,000

Life expectancy at birth: Male 76 years; Female 81 years

Official language: Danish

Ethnic composition: Scandinavian, Inuit, Faroese, German, Turkish, Iranian, Somali

Religious affiliation: Evangelical Lutheran 95%, other Christian (includes Protestant and Roman Catholic) 3%, Muslim 2%

Currency: Danish krone (DKK)

GDP: US$197.8 billion; per capita US$36,000

Natural resources: Petroleum, natural gas, fish, salt, limestone, chalk, stone, gravel and sand

Forests cover around 10 per cent of the land area, mainly as plantations of coniferous trees. The major river in Denmark is the Gudenå, which flows for a total length of 158 km (98 miles) from its source in the eastern centre of Jutland to Randers Fjord on the east coast.

Denmark's climate is influenced by winds from the Atlantic Ocean, the Arctic Ocean and Eastern Europe. This makes its weather very changeable, but on the whole it has a mild climate with regular rainfall throughout the year. Summer temperatures reach an average maximum of just 16°C (60°F) in July and, although there is snow during the winter months, the average temperature only drops to an average of 0°C (32°F).

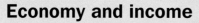 Denmark is a world leader in wind power and, along with other EU nations, is investing in offshore wind farms to help cut carbon emissions and reduce climate change.

Economy and income

The service sector makes up around three-quarters of all employment in Denmark, with tourism being a key industry. Manufacturing industries include food processing, pharmaceuticals, metals, transport and machinery. Denmark specialises in the production of modern wind turbines for generating electricity. Agriculture is important throughout much of Denmark and is focused on livestock (especially cows, pigs and chickens) and grains (wheat and barley). Denmark is one of the largest fish exporters in the world and has a very modern fleet.

Society

Most people in Denmark are of Danish origin, but there are small numbers of people with other ethnic origins including those who come from Germany, Poland, Turkey, Iraq, Iran, Bosnia and Somalia. Marriage in Denmark is less common than in other parts of Europe and up to half of all children are born to unmarried parents. Denmark has a very good welfare system, with benefits for all those who are unable to support themselves financially. This system is paid for by means of high taxes on income and goods.

Danish culture

Denmark is perhaps most famous for the children's writer Hans Christian Andersen who wrote many of the world's best-known fairy tales such 'The Ugly Duckling' and 'The Emperor's New Clothes'. Denmark is also known for its designers, including the architect and furniture designer Arne Jacobsen and Jørn Utzon (who designed the Sydney Opera House in Australia).

Ireland

When Ireland joined the EU in 1973 it was one of Europe's poorest nations, but membership has helped to transform it into a modern and wealthy economy. Increased European trade and EU funding have improved Ireland's transport and communications, and the Irish now enjoy a higher than average standard of living for the EU.

Geography

Ireland lies in the Atlantic Ocean to the west of Great Britain and is one of the most westerly nations in the Europe. It shares the island of Ireland with Northern Ireland, which is part of the UK. Most of Ireland is made up of lowlands and includes large areas of peat bog and several lakes.

Facts at a glance

Year of EU entry: 1973

Land area: 68,883 sq km (26,595 sq miles)

Climate: Temperate maritime; mild winters, cool summers; consistently humid; overcast about half the time

Highest point: Carrauntoohil 1,041 m (3,415 ft)

Lowest point: Atlantic Ocean 0 m (0 ft)

Population: 4.6 million

Urban population: 62%

Largest city: Dublin (capital) 1,099,000

Life expectancy at birth: Male 78 years; Female 82 years

Political system: Republic

Official languages: English, Irish

Ethnic composition: Irish 87.4%, other white 7.5%, Asian 1.3%, black 1.1%, mixed 1.1%, unspecified 1.6%

Religious affiliation: Roman Catholic 87.4%, Church of Ireland 2.9%, other Christian 1.9%, other 2.1%, unspecified 1.5%, none 4.2%

Currency: 1 euro = 100 cents

GDP: US$172.5 billion; per capita US$41,000

Natural resources: Natural gas, peat, copper, lead, zinc, silver, barite, gypsum, limestone, dolomite

▼ A typical rural scene in Ireland: cattle graze in a field in County Cork, in the south of the country.

IRELAND

There are several chains of low hills and mountains, including the Wicklow Mountains in the east and Macgillycuddy's Reeks in the south-west, which includes the country's highest point, Carrantuohill. The west coast is rugged, with many flooded river valleys. The east coast is gentler and has several large sandy beaches.

Ireland's climate is mainly mild and wet with warm moist air arriving from across the Atlantic Ocean to the west. There is little variation in temperature across the country, but the average annual rainfall in the west is over three times greater than in the east.

⬭ The O'Connell Bridge crosses the River Liffey in Dublin's busy city centre.

Economy and income

Ireland was traditionally a farming nation and farming remains important. Beef and dairy farming dominate and are major Irish exports. Some grains (wheat and barley) and root crops (mainly sugar beet and potatoes) are also grown. The modern economy is dominated by hi-tech industries. Ireland is one of the world's biggest software-producing nations and is home to the EU headquarters of many international computer companies. Financial services are important, but suffered greatly during the global recession of 2008–2010. In November 2010, the EU provided 67.5 billion euros to help strengthen the Irish economy.

Society

Many Irish people live outside Ireland, having left for the UK, America, Australia and elsewhere during the country's years of poverty. When Ireland's economy began to recover in the 1990s many of these emigrants began to return and the population grew quickly. Most of Ireland's people are of Irish origin, but EU membership has attracted immigrants from elsewhere in Europe and especially Eastern Europe. Smaller populations from Asian and African countries are also present in the larger towns and cities. Dublin is by far the biggest city, with around a quarter of the population living there.

Irish culture

Ireland is famous for its rich local culture, which includes traditional music, dance and a love of writing and poetry. These traditions are kept alive in local festivals that take place across the country and are popular with local people and tourists alike. Many well-known writers have come from Ireland, including W.B. Yeats, James Joyce, Samuel Beckett, Oscar Wilde and George Bernard Shaw. In recent times Ireland has produced many popular music acts such as U2, The Corrs and Van Morrison.

The UK

The UK is properly called the United Kingdom of Great Britain and Northern Ireland. It is made up of England, Scotland and Wales (these form Great Britain), and Northern Ireland, which covers the northernmost portion of the island of Ireland. The UK does not always agree with the EU and often takes different decisions. It chose not to adopt the euro as its currency, for example.

Geography

The UK is located to the west of mainland Europe in the North Sea. Its landscape is mostly made up of rolling hills and low mountains, but levels out into low plains in the east and southeast.

Facts at a glance

Year of EU entry: 1973

Land area: 241,930 sq km (93,410 sq miles)

Climate:
Temperate; more than half the days are overcast

Highest point: Ben Nevis 1,343 m (4,406 ft)

Lowest point:
The Fens -4 m (-13 ft)

Political system:
Constitutional monarchy

Population: 62 million

Urban population: 90%

Largest cities:
London (capital) 8,615,000
Birmingham 2,296,000
Manchester 2,253,000

Life expectancy at birth:
Male 78 years;
Female 82 years

Official language: English

Ethnic composition:
White (of which English 83.6%, Scottish 8.6%, Welsh 4.9%, Northern Irish 2.9%) 92.1%, black 2%, Indian 1.8%, Pakistani 1.3%, mixed 1.2%, other 1.6% (2001 census)

Religious affiliation:
Christian (Anglican, Roman Catholic, Presbyterian, Methodist) 71.6%, Muslim 2.7%, Hindu 1%, other 1.6%, unspecified or none 23.1%

Currency: British pound (GBP) £1 = 100 pence

GDP:
US$2.13 trillion; per capita US$34,800

Natural resources:
Coal, petroleum, natural gas, iron ore, lead, zinc, gold, tin, limestone, salt, clay, chalk, gypsum, potash, silica sand, slate, arable land

The stunning lakes and mountains of Snowdonia, in North Wales, form one of the UK's national parks. Many EU nations have similar protected areas.

Scotland and Wales are the most mountainous regions of the UK and the nation's highest peak, Ben Nevis, is in Scotland. The UK has the longest coastline in the EU and one of the longest in the world at around 31,368 km (19,491 miles). Nowhere in the UK is more than 113 km (70 miles) from the coastline.

The UK has a maritime climate, meaning that its winds and weather are heavily influenced by the seas surrounding it. Warm and mild air coming from across the Atlantic Ocean dominates weather in the UK. This means the west of England (facing the Atlantic) is generally wetter and warmer than the east. Eastern parts can be much colder than the west, particularly during the winter when cold winds blow in from Scandinavia.

⬤ A view across London shows modern architecture such as the 'Gherkin' (on the left) rising above the older city streets.

Society

In the 1950s, the UK began to invite immigrants from its former colonies in Africa, the Caribbean and Asia to move to the UK to take up jobs in its economy. Many settled in the UK, and they have since been joined by others from around the world including from other EU countries such as Ireland, Italy, Spain and Poland. This has made the UK a very multicultural society, especially in its larger towns and cities.

Economy and industry

The UK has one of the strongest economies in the EU and the world. It is heavily reliant on service industries and especially the financial and insurance industries. London is a major global banking centre and trades billions of dollars around the world every day. Industry and manufacturing have declined in the UK and many factories have closed and moved overseas where costs are lower. The UK still has a strong manufacturing sector, however, and specialises in hi-tech and precision engineering such as the manufacture of aircraft engines and wings. Farming and fishing are also still important sectors, but have become far more mechanised than in the past and so employ far fewer people.

English culture

The UK has produced many of the EU's most famous writers including William Shakespeare, Charles Dickens, Jane Austen, Geoffrey Chaucer and Robert Burns. This trend continues today with popular modern writers such as Ian Rankin, Roald Dahl, Michael Morpurgo and J.K. Rowling. The UK has often been a leader in popular culture with the music of the Beatles and the Sex Pistols, the art of Damien Hirst and Tracey Emin, and the mysterious street art of Banksy.

Greece

Greece lies in the far south-east of the EU region and is closer to Asia than to much of Europe. Famous for its ancient civilisation and the original home of the Olympic Games, it is also a modern industrial and service economy with a major tourist industry.

Geography

About four-fifths of Greece is mountainous, dominated by the Pindus Mountains in the north and the Peloponnese in the south. Greece's coastline is jagged and reaches far inland so that no point is further than 80 km (50 miles) from the coast. Greece has over 2,000 islands, making up about one-fifth of its area. They are divided into several groups including the Aegean, Ionian and Cyclades Islands.

◯ The Parthenon on the Acropolis in Athens is a world-famous symbol of the contribution made by the Ancient Greeks to modern science, culture and politics.

Facts at a glance

Year of EU entry: 1981

Land area: 130,647 sq km (50,443 sq miles)

Climate: Variable (see page 25)

Highest point: Mount Olympus 2,917 m (9,570 ft)

Lowest point: Mediterranean Sea 0 m (0 ft)

Political system: Republic

Population: 11.3 million

Urban population: 61%

Largest city:
Athens (capital) 3,257,000

Life expectancy at birth:
Male 77 years;
Female 83 years

Official language: Greek

Ethnic composition:
Greek 93%, other (foreign citizens) 7%

Religious affiliation:
Greek Orthodox 98%, Muslim 1.3%, other 0.7%

Currency:
1 euro = 100 cents

GDP:
US$333.4 billion; per capita US$31,000

Natural resources:
Lignite, petroleum, iron ore, bauxite, lead, zinc, nickel, magnesite, marble, salt, hydroelectric power potential

Greece has a Mediterranean climate that is generally hot and dry in the summer, with average temperatures of around 27°C (80°F). Winters are cooler, at around 6–12°C (43–54°F), and wetter, with snow falling on the higher ground. The western parts of the country receive around three times more rainfall than eastern and southern parts.

Economy and income

Greece is poorer than many EU nations and relies on only a few economic sectors. Shipping is one of its biggest industries and Greece has one of the world's largest merchant shipping fleets. Tourism makes up about 15 per cent of the national income, but it is a seasonal industry that slows down or closes in the winter. Another seasonal industry is farming and Greece is a major producer of fruits and nuts for export and of olives, used to make olive oil.

Nearly a fifth of the workforce in Greece is made up of immigrant workers, mostly in agriculture and low-skilled service, manufacturing and construction jobs. Incomes are about a third lower than the EU average and the Greek economy is less developed than others in the EU. As a result, Greece suffered more than other EU countries during the global recession of 2008–10. The Greek government has been forced to introduce dramatic spending cuts to help the economy recover.

Society

Ageing is a major issue for Greece, with 19.2 per cent of people over 65 years of age, compared to an EU average of 17.3 per cent. This is one reason why Greece has so many migrant workers. Greece's population includes people originating from Turkey, Albania, Macedonia, Armenia, Italy and Hungary. Ethnicity is not officially recorded and so many people consider themselves simply as Greek.

⬤ Santorini is one of many Greek islands that have become popular tourist destinations for people from across the EU and beyond.

Greek culture

Greece is best known for its ancient culture and philosophers such as Socrates, Aristotle and Plato. Alexander the Great was a famous Greek king whose explorations and military conquests in the 3rd century BCE built cultural links between Asia and Europe. Modern Greek culture has many leading names, including the film-maker Kostas Gavras, the composer Mikis Theodorakis and the Nobel Prize-winning poet Odysseus Elytis. Greek food is dominated by olive oil, salads, fish and goat meat.

Spain

Spain has benefited greatly from EU membership since 1986, with increased trade and EU support to develop infrastructure such as roads and railways.

Geography

Spain shares the Iberian Peninsula with Portugal to its west. The Pyrenees Mountains and the small state of Andorra form its other land borders with France in the north-east. Spain includes the Balearic Islands in the Mediterranean and the Canary Islands off the West African coast in the Atlantic Ocean. Mainland Spain is dominated by a highland plateau, called the Meseta Central. It is surrounded by low mountain chains, and the Central Sierra Mountains cross the Meseta diagonally from south-west to north-east.

Facts at a glance

Year of EU entry: 1986

Land area: 498,980 sq km (192,657 sq miles)

Climate: Variable (see page 27)

Highest point: Pico de Teide (Tenerife) 3,718 m (12,198 ft)

Lowest point: Atlantic Ocean 0 m (0 ft)

Political system: Constitutional monarchy

Population: 46.7 million

Urban population: 77%

Largest cities: Madrid (capital) 5,083,000 Barcelona 5,851,000

Life expectancy at birth: Male 78 years; Female 84 years

Official language: Spanish

Ethnic composition: Mixture of Mediterranean and Nordic types

Religious affiliation: Roman Catholic 94%, other 6%

Currency: 1 euro = 100 cents

GDP: US$1.36 trillion; per capita US$33,600

Natural resources: Coal, lignite, iron ore, copper, lead, zinc, uranium, tungsten, mercury, pyrites, magnesite, fluorspar, gypsum, sepiolite, kaolin, potash, hydroelectric power, arable land

⬤ Solar panels generate clean energy in the Spanish sunshine. Spain is a world leader in renewable energy technology and a major manufacturer of wind and solar power equipment.

The Ebro River in the north-east and the Guadalquivir River in the south-west are the major rivers and form depressions in the plateau. The main lowlands in Spain are coastal plains along the Mediterranean Sea.

Spain's size and varied landscape mean that it has a very complicated climate. A cool and dry mountain climate dominates the highlands, while coastal regions are influenced by warm and mild winds from the seas. Other regions have a temperate climate with few extremes, while the Canary Islands (off West Africa) enjoy a sub-tropical climate.

Economy and income

The Spanish economy is a mix of manufacturing, services and agriculture. Manufacturing includes telecommunications, biotechnology, electronics and pharmaceuticals, and consumer goods such as foodstuffs, clothing, shoes and furniture. A growing sector in Spain is the production of renewable energy using technologies such as solar and wind power. Banking, communications and tourism are the most important service sector industries. Tourism is especially important and Spain is where the modern package holiday began. Agriculture is less important than in the past and many small rural farms have closed or declined. Specialist products make an important contribution to the economy and include grapes (used for wine), olives, nuts, fruit (especially oranges), tomatoes and peppers.

Society

Spain has been invaded many times in its history and was also a nation of great explorers. This has given Spain connections throughout the world, as well as within the EU. Its population includes people from North Africa, South America, Eastern Europe and Asia, with the major cities being especially multicultural. Within Spain, the country is divided into 17 regions or communities, each with their own character and many with their own language. Catalonia, Valencia, Andalucia and the Basque Country are among the better known of these regions.

⬤ The Sagrada Familia in Barcelona, designed by Antonio Gaudí, is so complex that it will have taken over 100 years to build by the time it is finished in 2026.

Spanish culture

Spain's rich culture has produced many of Europe's most famous painters (such as Goya, Picasso and Dalí) and the author Cervantes, who wrote Don Quixote. Antonio Gaudí is a world-famous Spanish architect known for his bizarre-looking buildings and colourful mosaics. More recent cultural leaders from Spain include the film director Pedro Almodóvar, whose films have won many awards.

Portugal

Portugal makes up about one-sixth of the Iberian Peninsula and is the most westerly country in the EU. In the fifteenth and sixteenth centuries, Portugal was the world's wealthiest country, with an empire that included parts of the Americas, Africa and Asia. Today, however, its people are relatively poor – compared to the EU average.

Geography

Portugal is bordered to the north and east by Spain and to the south and west by the Atlantic Ocean. Portugal has a mountainous north and a lower southern region, divided by the Tagus River that flows south-west through Portugal to join the Atlantic near Lisbon. Southern Portugal has many sandy beaches, which have become popular as a European tourist destination.

PORTUGAL

Facts at a glance

Year of EU entry : 1986

Land area: 91,470 sq km (35,317 sq miles)

Climate: Maritime; temperate

Highest point:
Ponta do Pico in the Azores 2,351 m (7,713 ft)

Lowest point:
Atlantic Ocean 0 m (0ft)

Political system:
Republic

Population: 10.7 million

Urban population: 61%

Largest cities:
Lisbon (capital) 2,824,000
Porto 1,355,000

Life expectancy at birth:
Male 75 years;
Female 82 years

Official language:
Portuguese

Ethnic composition: Generally Mediterranean stock; citizens of black African descent who immigrated to mainland during decolonisation number fewer than 100,000; since 1990 Eastern Europeans have entered Portugal

Religious affiliation: Roman Catholic 84.5%, other Christian 2.2%, other 0.3%, unknown 9%, none 3.9%

Currency: 1 euro = 100 cents

GDP:
US$383.4 billion, per capita US$36,800

Natural resources:
Fish, forests (cork), iron ore, copper, zinc, tin, tungsten, silver, gold, uranium, marble, clay, gypsum, salt, arable land, hydroelectric power

 Portugal receives around 12.5 million tourists each year. They come to enjoy coastal resorts such as Ferragudo harbour, shown here, in the Algarve.

Portugal's climate is most influenced by the Atlantic Ocean, which brings warm temperatures and regular rainfall to much of the country. The north and west are wetter than the east and south, however, with rainfall in the extreme south being around 500 mm (20 inches) per year, compared to 2,000 mm (80 inches) in the far north. Temperatures follow a similar pattern, with the south being a few degrees warmer than the north and everywhere cooler at higher altitudes.

Economy and income

About a third of Portugal's land is used for farming. The main crops are grains such as wheat and barley, potatoes, grapes (for wine), and fresh produce, especially tomatoes, apples and oranges. Forestry supports a paper and pulp industry and Portugal is one of the world's leading cork producers. EU money for new boats and improved port facilities has helped to revive Portugal's fishing industry and provide fish for local consumption and export. Manufacturing and industry make up around a quarter of the economy and Portugal produces a wide range of goods, including cement, petrochemicals, wood products, clothes, shoes, furniture, foodstuffs, electronics, chemicals and vehicles. Portugal's service sector accounts for most income and employment. Tourism is an especially important sector that has seen rapid growth since the early 1990s.

Society

Most people in Portugal are of Portuguese origin but there are some from former Portuguese colonies (including Brazil, which shares the Portuguese language). There is a Chinese population and a range of people from other parts of the EU, mostly employed as temporary workers in tourism or agriculture. Portugal's population remains more rural than many other EU nations, but the general trend is of people moving to the cities, especially the industrial centres of Lisbon, Setubal and Porto.

⬥ Cork trees are native to the Portuguese landscape. Their bark is harvested to make cork products such as floor tiles and bottle corks for the wine industry.

Portuguese culture

Portugal has a vibrant culture and has made important contributions to European art, architecture, film and literature. It is well known for its folk dance and music (known as *fado*) and when one of its most famous *fadistas* (*fado* singers), Amália Rodrigues, died in 1999 there were three days of national mourning. Portugal also specialises in *azulejos* – glazed decorative tiles. These beautiful works can be seen on the front of many of the country's greatest buildings and are celebrated in the National Tile Museum in Lisbon.

Austria

Austria is at the heart of south central Europe, bordered by eight other countries, six of them in the EU. Its southern and western regions are dominated by the Alps, whose stunning scenery makes Austria a popular tourist destination. In the east, the River Danube (Europe's second-longest river) is the main feature and passes through the capital Vienna, before entering Slovakia to the east.

Manufacturing and industry make up around 30 per cent of the Austrian economy, and the country has a reputation for the high-quality design and manufacture of power stations, chemical plants, steelworks and heavy machinery. Its highly skilled engineering workforce is in global demand. Tourism is another key industry. Austria's world-famous cultural contributors include the composers Mozart and Schubert, the philosopher Sigmund Freud and the artist Gustav Klimt.

Facts at a glance

Year of EU entry: 1995

Land area: 82,445 sq km (31,832 sq miles)

Climate:
Temperate; continental, cloudy; cold winters with frequent rain and some snow in lowlands and snow in mountains; moderate summers

Highest point:
Grossglockner 3,798 m (12,461ft)

Lowest point:
Neusiedler See 115 m (377 ft)

Political system:
Federal republic

Population: 8.4 million

Urban population: 68%

Largest city:
Vienna (capital) 1,706,000

Life expectancy at birth:
Male 77 years;
Female 83 years

Official language:
German

Ethnic composition:
Austrians 91.1%, former Yugoslavs 4% (includes Croatians, Slovenes, Serbs, and Bosniaks), Turks 1.6%, Germans 0.9%, other or unspecified 2.4%

Religious affiliation:
Roman Catholic 73.6%, Protestant 4.7%, Muslim 4.2%, other 3.5%, unspecified 2%, none 12%

Currency:
1 euro = 100 cents

GDP:
US$321.8 billion; per capita US$39,200

Natural resources:
Oil, coal, lignite, timber, iron ore, copper, zinc, antimony, magnesite, tungsten, graphite, salt, hydroelectric power

The Alps of Austria are used for dairy farming, but also provide a popular location for walking in the summer and skiing in winter.

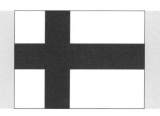

Finland

Facts at a glance

Year of EU entry: 1995

Land area: 303,815 sq km (117,304 sq miles)

Climate:
Cold temperate; potentially subarctic but comparatively mild because of moderating influence of the North Atlantic Current, Baltic Sea, and lakes

Highest point: Haltiatunturi 1,328 m (4,357 ft)

Lowest point:
Baltic Sea 0 m (0 ft)

Population: 5.3 million

Urban population: 85%

Largest city:
Helsinki (capital) 1,117,000

Life expectancy at birth:
Male 76 years;
Female 83 years

Political system:
Republic

Official languages:
Finnish, Swedish

Ethnic composition:
Finn 93.4%, Swede 5.6%, Russian 0.5%, Estonian 0.3%, Roma (Gypsy) 0.1%, Sami (indigenous inhabitants) 0.1%

Religious affiliation:
Lutheran Church of Finland 82.5%, Orthodox Church 1.1%, other Christian 1.1%, other 0.1%, none 15.1%

Currency: 1 euro = 100 cents

GDP: US$178.8 billion; per capita US$34,100

Natural resources:
Timber, iron ore, copper, lead, zinc, chromite, nickel, gold, silver, limestone

Finland is a land of largely unspoilt wilderness. Its northern regions are so far north that it experiences around ten weeks of constant daylight in the summer, and around eight weeks of constant darkness in the winter. It is a land of forests – with about 60,000 lakes. It is mainly low-lying but rises towards the centre and the north-west, where it borders Norway and Sweden.

Finland only joined the EU in 1995, and adopted the euro as its currency in 1999. It has a strong and modern economy based on forestry and wood products, metal processing, engineering, telecommunications and electronics. It is a world leader in mobile phone technology. Finland's relatively small population is mainly Finnish, but includes a significant number of Swedish people and a smaller number of Eastern Europeans.

🔻 This view of Helsinki, the Finnish capital, shows the city's port area and its famous cathedral.

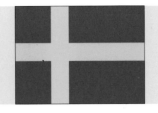

Sweden

Sweden is one of the northernmost nations in the EU. Around 60 per cent of the country is mountainous and covered in forests. Elsewhere the landscape is made up of gentle hills and fertile plains. Sweden is also a land of water, with over 90,000 lakes.

Sweden's economy is a mix of services, manufacturing and mining, and it has internationally famous brands including Volvo, Saab and IKEA. EU membership has made it easier for Swedish companies like these to trade with other European nations.

Sweden is one of the world's wealthiest countries, with a strong welfare system providing generous education and health benefits, paid for by high taxes. Most Swedes live in the main cities, in the south of the country, and enjoy a wide range of art and culture. One of the world's most successful pop groups, Abba, came from Sweden in the 1970s.

⊙ Stockholm is one of the best-preserved cities in the EU and its residents enjoy a standard of living that is among the highest in the world.

Facts at a glance

Year of EU entry: 1995

Land area: 410,335 sq km (158, 431 sq miles)

Climate: Temperate in south, with cold, cloudy winters and cool, partly cloudy summers; subarctic in north

Highest point: Kebnekaise 2,111 m (6,926 ft)

Lowest point: Bay of Lake Hammarsjon (reclaimed) -2.4 m (-8 ft)

Political system: Constitutional monarchy

Population: 9.3 million

Urban population: 85%

Largest city: Stockholm (capital) 1,285,000

Life expectancy at birth: Male 79 years; Female 83 years

Official language: Swedish

Ethnic composition: Swedes 90%, Finns 3%, Sami (indigenous inhabitants) 0.15%

Religious affiliation: Lutheran 87%, other (includes Roman Catholic, Orthodox, Baptist, Muslim, Jewish, and Buddhist) 13%

Currency: Swedish kronor (SEK) 1 krona (kr) = 100 ore

GDP: US$331.4 billion; per capita US$36,600

Natural resources: Iron ore, copper, lead, zinc, gold, silver, tungsten, uranium, arsenic, feldspar, timber, hydroelectric power

Cyprus

Facts at a glance

Year of EU entry: 2004

Land area: 9,241 sq km (3,568 sq miles)

Climate: Temperate; Mediterranean with hot, dry summers and cool winters

Highest point: Mount Olympus 1,951 m (6,401 ft)

Lowest point: Mediterranean Sea 0 m (0 ft)

Political system: Republic

Population: 0.8 million

Urban population: 70%

Largest city: Nicosia/Lefkosia (capital) <750,000

Life expectancy at birth: Male 75 years; Female 81 years

Official languages: Greek, English

Ethnic composition: Greek 77%, Turkish 18%, other 5% (2001)

Religious affiliation: Greek Orthodox 78%, Muslim 18%, other (includes Maronite and Armenian Apostolic) 4%

Currency: 1 euro = 100 cents

GDP: US$ 22.8 billion; per capita US$21,000

Natural resources: Copper, pyrites, asbestos, gypsum, timber, salt, marble, clay earth pigment

▶ Cyprus is located along important trade routes through the Mediterranean. The castle and harbour in Paphos provide evidence of Cyprus's long-standing relationship with the sea.

Cyprus is the third-largest island in the Mediterranean and lies about 65 km (40 miles) south of Turkey. It is a mountainous island with coastal plains and a fertile centre. It has a Mediterranean climate, with hot, dry summers and wetter and cooler winters.

In 1974, the island split into the (mainly Greek) Republic of Cyprus in the south and the (mainly Turkish) Turkish Republic of Northern Cyprus in the northern third. The Republic of Cyprus is the internationally recognised government and the part of the island that belongs in the EU. It is wealthier than the north, with an economy that is based on trade as well as shipping, banking and tourism. The north of the island still relies far more heavily on agriculture for its income and has an entirely separate economy from the south.

Talks are being held between the southern and northern governments of Cyprus to try to unite the island as a single country.

Czech Republic

Until 1993, the Czech Republic was part of Czechoslovakia, together with Slovakia to the east. Around 95 per cent of the Czech Republic is hilly or mountainous, with the lowland regions being mostly in river valleys and along the border with Poland to the north-east. The climate is continental, with cold winters and warm or hot summers. Temperatures vary greatly according to altitude, and rainfall also varies, with the north receiving around three times more precipitation than central areas.

Czechoslovakia is highly industrialised. The iron and steel industries are especially important and help other key sectors such as engineering and the manufacture of heavy machinery. The Czech car company Skoda is now a major European brand and has benefited greatly from improvements in trade due to EU membership. Agriculture is based on grains, livestock and dairy production, and Czech beers are world-famous. The capital, Prague, has become one of the most popular tourist destinations in Europe.

Facts at a glance

Year of EU entry: 2004

Land area: 77,247 sq km (29,825 sq miles)

Climate: Temperate; cool summers; cold, cloudy, humid winters

Highest point: Snezka 1,602 m (5,256 ft)

Lowest point: Elbe River 115 m (377 ft)

Population: 10.4 million

Urban population: 74%

Largest city: Prague (capital) 1,162,000

Life expectancy at birth: Male 74 years; Female 80 years

Official language: Czech

Political system: Parliamentary democracy

Ethnic composition: Czech 90.4%, Moravian 3.7%, Slovak 1.9%, other 4%

Religious affiliation: Roman Catholic 26.8%, Protestant 2.1%, other 3.3%, unspecified 8.8%, unaffiliated 59%

Currency: 1 euro = 100 cents

GDP: US$254.1 billion; per capita US$24,900

Natural resources: Hard coal, soft coal, kaolin, clay, graphite, timber

◀ This view of Prague shows the Charles Bridge, which crosses the Vltava River.

Estonia

Estonia became independent from the Soviet Union in 1991, but remains linked to Russia. It is a small country of gentle hills and forests that includes many lakes and rivers and around 1,500 islands. It is surrounded by the Baltic Sea, except for its eastern border with Russia and the southern border with Latvia.

Estonia is a major producer of oil shale, wood products (including furniture, matches and plywood) and processed food, and also manufactures machinery, textiles and shoes, and electrical and telecommunications equipment. Agricultural products include potatoes, barley and livestock (mainly pigs and cattle).

Since 1991, the service sector has grown in Estonia, particularly tourism. Besides Russians, Estonia is also home to people originating from Ukraine, Belarus and Finland. Estonia has benefited greatly from joining other EU nations in major policy areas such as energy supply and climate change; 85 per cent of Estonian residents are in favour of its EU membership.

⬤ The medieval walled city of Tallinn is now a popular tourist destination in Estonia.

Facts at a glance

Year of EU entry: 2004

Land area: 42,388 sq km (16,366 sq miles)

Climate:
Maritime; wet, moderate winters, cool summers

Highest point: Suur Munamägi 318 m (1,043 ft)

Lowest point:
Baltic Sea 0 m (0 ft)

Political system:
Parliamentary republic

Population: 1.3 million

Urban population: 70%

Largest city:
Tallinn (capital) <750,000

Life expectancy at birth:
Male 68 years;
Female 79 years

Official language:
Estonian

Ethnic composition:
Estonian 68.7%, Russian 25.6%, Ukrainian 2.1%, Belarusian 1.2%, Finn 0.8%, other 1.6%

Religious affiliation:
Evangelical Lutheran 13.6%, Orthodox 12.8%, other Christian (including Methodist, Seventh-Day Adventist, Roman Catholic, Pentecostal) 1.4%, unaffiliated 34.1%, other and unspecified 32%, none 6.1%

Currency:
1 euro = 100 cents

GDP:
US$24 billion; per capita US$18,500

Natural resources:
Oil shale, peat, phosphorite, clay, limestone, sand, dolomite, arable land, sea mud

Hungary

Hungary is mostly made up of fertile plains, with low hills and mountains to the north and west, and the Transdanubia and Northern Mountains that divide Hungary from south-west to north-east. The Danube is Hungary's longest river and divides Buda and Pest, which together make up the capital city of Budapest.

Agriculture is less important than in the past, but has helped Hungary to be self-sufficient in food. Wheat, maize, sugar beet, potatoes, sunflowers and fruits are among the major crops. In terms of minerals, Hungary is a major producer and exporter of bauxite, which is used to make aluminium.

Manufacturing industries include chemicals, food processing, paper and wood products, heavy machinery, telecommunications and vehicle production. In 2010 a Hungarian aluminium factory suffered a major disaster when waste sludge leaked from a store into the environment. The EU authorities helped Hungary to control the accident and prevent the pollution from spreading to neighbouring EU countries.

Facts at a glance

Year of EU entry: 2004

Land area: 89,608 sq km (34,599 sq miles)

Climate:
Temperate; cold, cloudy, humid winters; warm summers

Highest point:
Kékes 1,014 m (3,327 ft)

Lowest point:
Tisza River 78 m (256 ft)

Political system:
Parliamentary democracy

Population: 10 million

Urban population: 68%

Largest city:
Budapest (capital) 1,706,000

Life expectancy at birth:
Male 71 years; Female 79 years

Official language:
Hungarian

Ethnic composition:
Hungarian 92.3%, Roma 1.9%, other or unknown 5.8%

Religious affiliation:
Roman Catholic 51.9%, Calvinist 15.9%, Lutheran 3%, Greek Catholic 2.6%, other Christian 1%, other 25.6%

Currency: Forint

GDP: US$186 billion; per capita US$18,800

Natural resources: Bauxite, coal, natural gas, arable land

▶ These vineyards in Badacsony, in Hungary's northern highlands, produce popular white wines.

Latvia

Latvia is in the middle of the Baltic States located between Estonia to the north and Lithuania to the south. Its landscape is a mix of flat plains and gentle hills. Forests cover around a third of the country and other features include peat bogs, meadows and numerous rivers that drain into the Baltic Sea. The largest of these is the Western Dvina River, which flows 357 km (222 miles) across Latvia. The climate is cool and rainy, with a short summer and a long winter, when temperatures can drop to -40°C (-40°F).

The Latvian economy is based on timber products, machinery, textiles, food processing, chemicals, pharmaceuticals and tourism. Finance and other business services are increasingly important and have expanded as Latvia has traded more with other EU nations. Only around 60 per cent of the population is actually Latvian, with Russian, Belorussian, Ukrainian and Polish people making up the balance. Latvian culture is frequently celebrated through folk songs and festivals.

⬥ This view of central Riga shows the town hall (right) and Sacred Peter's Church (left).

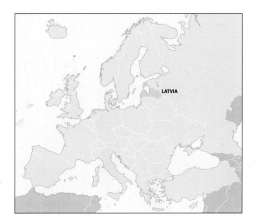

Facts at a glance

Year of EU entry: 2004

Land area: 62,249 sq km (24,034 sq miles)

Climate:
Maritime; wet, moderate winters

Highest point: Galzina Kalns 312 m (1,024 ft)

Lowest point:
Baltic Sea 0 m (0 ft)

Political system:
Parliamentary democracy

Population: 2.2 million

Urban population: 68%

Largest city:
Riga (capital) <750,000

Life expectancy at birth:
Male 67 years;
Female 78 years

Official language:
Latvian

Ethnic composition:
Latvian 59.3%, Russian 27.8%, Belarusian 3.6%, Ukrainian 2.5%, Polish 2.4%, Lithuanian 1.3%, other 3.1%

Religious affiliation:
Lutheran 19.6%, Orthodox 15.3%, other Christian 1%, other 0.4%, unspecified 63.7%

Currency: Lats (LVL) 1 lats = 100 santimi

GDP:
US$32.2 billion; per capita US$14,400

Natural resources:
Peat, limestone, dolomite, amber, hydroelectric power, timber, arable land

Lithuania

Lithuania is the southernmost, largest and most populated of the Baltic States. Almost one-third of the country is covered in forests, and water is a major feature – with around 3,000 lakes and 758 rivers. The climate is generally cool and damp.

About 84 per cent of the people are ethnic Lithuanians, and most others are from Poland or Russia. Just over two-thirds of the population lives in towns or cities. This proportion is growing, as farming becomes less important and is replaced by services such as banking, retail and tourism.

Major industries include food processing, textiles, chemicals, communications technology and oil and gas refining. Since joining the EU, Lithuania has had more investment from other EU nations and an increase in tourism.

⬤ These girls were among the thousands who took part in the Europeade 2009 Festival of European Folk Culture in Klaipeda, Lithuania.

LITHUANIA

Facts at a glance

Year of EU entry: 2004

Land area: 62,680 sq km (24,201 sq miles)

Climate:
Transitional, between maritime and continental; wet, moderate winters and summers

Highest point:
Aukštojas 294 m (965 ft)

Lowest point:
Baltic Sea 0 m (0 ft)

Political system:
Parliamentary democracy

Population:
3.3 million

Urban population: 67%

Largest city:
Vilnius (capital) <750,000

Life expectancy at birth:
Male 70 years;
Female 80 years

Official language:
Lithuanian

Ethnic composition:
Lithuanian 84%, Polish 6.1%, Russian 4.9%, Belarusian 1.1%, other or unspecified 3.9%

Religious affiliation:
Roman Catholic 79%, Russian Orthodox 4.1%, Protestant (including Lutheran and Evangelical Christian Baptist) 1.9%, other or unspecified 5.5%, none 9.5%

Currency: Litas (Lt) 1 litas = 100 centai

GDP:
US$55.1 billion; per capita US$15,500

Natural resources:
Peat, arable land, amber

Malta

Facts at a glance

Year of EU entry: 2004

Land area: 316 sq km
(122 sq miles)

Climate:
Mediterranean; mild, rainy
winters; hot, dry summers

Highest point:
Ta'Dmejrek 253 m (830 ft))

Lowest point:
Mediterranean Sea 0 m (0 ft)

Population: 0.4 million

Urban population: 95%

Largest city:
Valletta (capital) <750,000

Life expectancy at birth:
Male 77 years;
Female 82 years

Official languages:
Maltese, English

Political system: Republic

Ethnic composition:
Maltese (descended from
ancient peoples of North
Africa and Middle East with
strong elements of Italian and
other Mediterranean stock)

Religious affiliation:
Roman Catholic 98%

Currency: 1 euro = 100 cents

GDP:
US$9.8 billion; per capita
US$24,300

Natural resources:
Limestone, salt, arable land

With a population of just 0.4 million, Malta has the smallest population of all EU members. Its people are spread across three of the seven islands that make up the country – Malta, Gozo and Comino. Malta is located in the Mediterranean Sea, south of Italy, and enjoys a warm and sunny climate for much of the year. Its landscape is mostly low and rocky, with sea cliffs along much of the coastline. Farming is small-scale in Malta and focused on producing food for consumption such as potatoes, vegetables and fruits. Olives and grapes (for wine) have been grown in greater quantities since the 1990s.

Malta's main industry has traditionally been shipbuilding and ship repairs, but since joining the EU the Maltese economy has become much more diverse. Software manufacture, computer electronics, automotive and aircraft parts, and pharmaceuticals are among the major new industries. Tourism is one of the most important service industries in Malta, but the fragile islands have been damaged by the demands of thousands of visitors so the government is now trying to promote lower-impact ecotourism to protect the environment.

▼ Colourful, traditional fishing boats are seen here against the backdrop of Marsaxlokk village in Malta.

Poland

Poland is the largest and most populous of the former Soviet-controlled countries to join the EU. The country is mostly made up of lowlands, but rises to the Carpathian and Sudeten Mountains along its border with Slovakia and the Czech Republic. The Vistula River stretches for 1,047 km (651 miles) from south to north, passing through the capital Warsaw and entering the Baltic Sea near the port of Gdansk. Poland has cold and snowy winters, and warm and wet summers.

Poland's natural resources include coal and sulphur. Salt is also important and has been mined at the Wieliczka salt mine near Kraków for over 700 years. The mine is a world heritage site because it contains a village beneath the ground entirely made of salt!

Poland produces a range of timber products, textiles, chemicals, machinery, electrical items, foodstuffs and consumer goods. Services have grown rapidly since the 1990s and since joining the EU, especially banking, retail, tourism and leisure.

Facts at a glance

Year of EU entry: 2004

Land area: 304,255 sq km (117,474 sq miles)

Climate:
Temperate with cold, cloudy, moderately severe winters with frequent precipitation; mild, showery summers

Highest point:
Rysy 2,499 m (8,199 ft)

Lowest point: Near Raczki Elbaskie -2 m (-7 ft)

Political system: Republic

Population: 38.1 million

Urban population: 61%

Largest city:
Warsaw (capital) 1,712,000

Life expectancy at birth:
Male 72 years;
Female 80 years

Official language: Polish

Ethnic composition:
Polish 96.7%, German 0.4%, Belarusian 0.1%, Ukrainian 0.1%, other and unspecified 2.7%

Religious affiliation:
Roman Catholic 89.8% (about 75% practising), Eastern Orthodox 1.3%, Protestant 0.3%, other 0.3%, unspecified 8.3%

Currency: Zloty (PLN) 1 PLN = 100 groszy

GDP:
US$689.3 billion; per capita US$17,900

Natural resources:
Coal, sulphur, copper, natural gas, silver, lead, salt, amber, arable land

◀ Kraków's beautiful architecture makes it an important tourist destination. This is the Market Square in the centre of the city.

Slovakia

Facts at a glance

Year of EU entry: 2004

Land area: 48,105 sq km (18,573 sq miles)

Climate:
Temperate; cool summers; cold, cloudy, humid winters

Highest point: Gerlachovsky Stit 2,655 m (8,711 ft)

Lowest point:
Bodrok River 94 m (308 ft)

Political system:
Parliamentary democracy

Population: 5.4 million

Urban population: 55%

Largest city:
Bratislava (capital) <750,000

Life expectancy at birth:
Male 72 years;
Female 80 years

Official language: Slovak

Ethnic composition:
Slovak 85.8%, Hungarian 9.7%, Roma 1.7%, Ruthenian/Ukrainian 1%, other and unspecified 1.8%

Religious affiliation:
Roman Catholic 68.9%, Protestant 10.8%, Greek Catholic 4.1%, other or unspecified 3.2%, none 13%

Currency: 1 euro = 100 cents

GDP:
US$115.1 billion; per capita US$21,100

Natural resources:
Brown coal and lignite; small amounts of iron ore, copper and manganese ore; salt; arable land

Slovakia is the eastern part of the former Czechoslovakia and only became an independent nation in 1993. Its landscape is dominated by the Carpathian Mountains, which are a popular winter sports destination.

The lowlands in the south-west of Slovakia are the main farming region, with wheat, barley, sugar beet and maize being the major crops. In the less fertile mountain regions, sheep farming is the main activity.

The Slovak Ore Mountains in south central Slovakia contain high-grade iron ore that is used in the steel industry. Copper, manganese, lead and zinc are also mined in this region. Slovakia's manufacturing industry produces automobiles, machinery, steel, ceramics, textiles, foodstuffs and chemicals.

Investment in Slovakia more than doubled following EU membership with large companies such as the French car manufacturer Peugeot-Citroen opening new factories there.

⬥ Orava Castle, one of Slovakia's most famous castles, dates back to the thirteenth century.

SLOVAKIA

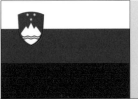

Slovenia

⬆ A horse rider enjoys the view in Triglav National Park, in north-west Slovenia, a popular area for tourists.

Slovenia was created in 1991 as the former Yugoslavia broke up into several new nations. Its northern region shares the Alps with Italy to the west and Austria to the north. Much of the rest of the country is also mountainous, with the only real lowland area being in the north-east along the border with Hungary. Slovenia has a short coastline of around 47 km (29 miles) on the Adriatic Sea to the west. The country's port city of Koper is located here.

Around three-fifths of Slovenia is covered in forests, and timber products are an important part of the economy. The main agricultural produce includes wheat, maize, barley, sugar beet, potatoes, apples and pears. Pigs, cattle and sheep are also kept and there is a small wine industry. Slovenia joined the EU in 2004 and adopted the euro as its currency in 2007. This has helped it to attract international investment and create new manufacturing jobs, producing automobiles, pharmaceuticals and electronics, mostly for export.

Facts at a glance

Year of EU entry: 2004

Land area: 20,151 sq km (7,780 sq miles)

Climate:
Mediterranean climate on the coast, continental climate with mild to hot summers and cold winters in the plateaux and valleys to the east

Highest point:
Triglav 2,864 m (9,396 ft)

Lowest point:
Adriatic Sea 0 m (0 ft)

Population: 2.0 million

Urban population: 50%

Largest city:
Ljubljana (capital) <750,000

Life expectancy at birth:
Male 73 years;
Female 81 years

Political system:
Parliamentary republic

Official language: Slovenian

Ethnic composition:
Slovene 83.1%, Serb 2%, Croat 1.8%, Bosniak 1.1%, other or unspecified 12%

Religious affiliation:
Catholic 57.8%, Muslim 2.4%, Orthodox 2.3%, other Christian 0.9%, unaffiliated 3.5%, other or unspecified 23%, none 10.1%

Currency: 1 euro = 100 cents

GDP:
US$55.5 billion; per capita US$27,700

Natural resources:
Lignite coal, lead, zinc, building stone, hydroelectric power, forests

Bulgaria

Facts at a glance

Year of EU entry: 2007

Land area: 108,489 sq km (41,888 sq miles)

Climate: Temperate; cold, damp winters; hot, dry summers

Highest point: Musala 2,925 m (9,596 ft)

Lowest point: Black Sea 0 m (0 ft)

Political system: Parliamentary democracy

Population: 7.6 million

Urban population: 72%

Largest city: Sofia (capital) 1,192,000

Life expectancy at birth: Male 70 years; Female 77 years

Official language: Bulgarian

Ethnic composition: Bulgarian 83.9%, Turk 9.4%, Roma 4.7%, other 2% (including Macedonian, Armenian, Tatar, Circassian)

Religious affiliation: Bulgarian Orthodox 82.6%, Muslim 12.2%, other Christian 1.2%, other 4%

Currency: Lev (BGN) 1 BGN = 100 stotinki

GDP: US$47.1 billion; per capita US$12,500

Natural resources: Bauxite, copper, lead, zinc, coal, timber, arable land

This aerial view of Primorsko Bay shows some of the rapid development that has taken place in recent years along Bulgaria's coast.

Bulgaria is located towards the south-eastern edge of Europe, bordering Greece and Turkey to the south and the Black Sea to the east. Its northern border with Romania follows the course of the Danube River as it flows west to east before draining into the Black Sea.

Bulgarian agriculture mainly focuses on cereals such as wheat, maize, barley, oats and rye. Sunflower seeds and tobacco are also grown and tomatoes and grapes are grown for export. Livestock rearing (cattle, pigs and sheep) and forestry are important. Coal is the main natural resource, but there are also reserves of iron ore, bauxite, copper, zinc, salt, limestone, kaolin, gypsum and other minerals.

Manufacturing is dominated by food processing and Bulgaria is a major exporter of foodstuffs to the EU. Tourism is one of the fastest-growing parts of the economy and has been greatly helped by EU membership and increased flights to other EU nations. Visitors are mainly attracted by Bulgaria's Black Sea beaches, scenic mountains and historic cities.

Romania

Located in south-east Europe, Romania is split between the Carpathian Mountains and highlands of the north and the southern plains of the Danube River as it flows along the border with Bulgaria to the Black Sea. Close to the Danube, the land is marshy and a haven for wildlife, and in some areas this land has been drained to create fertile farmland. The main crops include cereals such as wheat, maize, barley and rye, and Romania is also known for its vegetables and its orchards. It is also a major European wine producer.

Manufacturing and industry is focused on natural resources, including oil, natural gas, coal, iron, copper and bauxite, petrochemicals and engineering goods. The textiles, clothing and electronics industries have grown since the 1990s and were helped by Romania joining the EU in 2007. Tourism is also a growing sector that has been greatly helped by low-cost flights between Romania and other parts of Europe.

◯ A ski-tour in the Carpathian Mountains is just one of many new forms of tourism in Romania.

Facts at a glance

Year of EU entry: 2007

Land area: 229,891 sq km (88,761 sq miles)

Climate:
Temperate; cold, cloudy winters with frequent snow and fog; sunny summers with frequent showers and thunderstorms

Highest point: Moldoveanu 2,544 m (8,346 ft)

Lowest point:
Black Sea 0 m (0 ft)

Population: 21.3 million

Urban population: 58%

Largest city:
Bucharest (capital) 1,934,000

Life expectancy at birth:
Male 70 years;
Female 77 years

Official language: Romanian

Political system: Republic

Ethnic composition:
Romanian 89.5%, Hungarian 6.6%, Roma 2.5%, Ukrainian 0.3%, German 0.3%, Russian 0.2%, Turkish 0.2%, other 0.4%

Religious affiliation:
Eastern Orthodox 86.8%, Protestant 7.5%, Roman Catholic 4.7%, other 0.9%, none 0.1%

Currency: Leu (RON) 1 leu = 100 bani

GDP: US$253.3 billion; per capita US$11,500

Natural resources:
Petroleum (reserves declining), timber, natural gas, coal, iron ore, salt, arable land, hydroelectric power

Future applicants

The success of the EU in increasing trade between members and reducing the cost of business has made it very attractive to European countries that have not yet joined. Croatia, Turkey, Iceland and the former Yugoslav Republic of Macedonia are four candidate nations that are currently negotiating with the EU to become members.

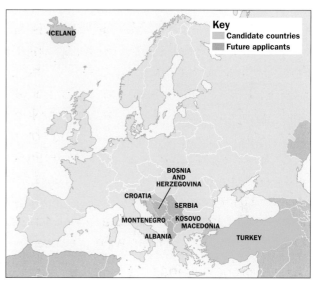

To join the EU, countries must ensure that they meet various criteria agreed by EU members. These include issues such as the management of the economy, the rights and freedoms of people living there, and the protection of the environment. Existing EU nations must be content for new members to join and this can involve a long negotiation process. Talks between Turkey and the EU, for example, began in 1959 and Turkey applied for full membership in 1987. One of the problems affecting Turkey's entry to the EU is the divided island of Cyprus (see page 33), the northern part of which is controlled by Turkey. Southern Cyprus joined the EU in 2004 but Turkey has failed to fully recognise the official Cypriot government of the south. This is a major obstacle to Turkey joining the EU, but talks continue to overcome this and other barriers.

A further five countries in the Balkan region of Europe are potential members of the EU in the future. They are Albania, Bosnia and Herzegovina, Kosovo, Montenegro and Serbia.

▼ Gjirokastra, in Albania, is a UNESCO World Heritage Town and a place that could potentially attract more visitors if Albania were to join the EU.

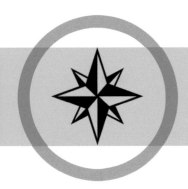

Glossary

civilisation society that is highly organised

coniferous trees trees with thin needle-like leaves that produce cones; many are fast growing and evergreen

constitutional monarchy political system where the head of state is a king or queen, but where their powers are limited by a constitution

criteria set of rules or standards that must be met, such as those needed to become an EU member

culture way of life and traditions of a particular group of people

democracy political system where people vote for their government representatives

economy way in which trade and money are controlled by a country

empire countries, peoples or areas under the authority of a single ruler or ruling country

engineering science of designing, constructing and maintaining buildings, machines and other things

ethnicity belonging to a group of people defined by common characteristics such as language and skin colour

export to sell goods or services to another country

fertile describes land or soil that can support the growth of crops

GDP total value of goods and services produced by a country, measured over a year

human rights principles such as the right to food and shelter, which are protected by international laws

hydroelectric power electricity made using the power of water

immigrant someone who moves to a country that is not their country of origin or birth

import to buy goods or services from another country

manufacturing making something or many things, using machinery

microelectronics designing and building extremely small electronic circuits

multicultural describes a society made up of people from many different countries, ethnic groups, language groups or religions

negotiation process of discussing something to reach an agreement

peninsula piece of land jutting out into the sea

petrochemicals products, such as petrol or paraffin, made from petroleum or natural gas

pharmaceuticals manufacture, preparation or sale of drugs used in medicine

plateau wide area of flat land high up in hills or mountains

precipitation any moisture that falls to the ground, including rain, snow, sleet and hail

recession period in which a country's economy declines instead of growing

republic state with elected representatives who form a government

service sector services such as healthcare, education, retail and leisure

subarctic region bordering the Arctic Circle

temperate describing a climate that has average temperatures with no major extremes throughout the year

tributary stream or river that flows into a larger stream or river

United Nations some nations working together for peace and development, based on the principles of justice, human dignity and well-being

Topic web

Use this topic web to explore EU themes in different areas of your curriculum.

Design and Technology

Imagine that the EU decided to create a new flag. Look at the current flags of the EU nations and work out your own design for a new EU flag.

Science

European scientists have made some of the world's most important scientific discoveries. Draw up a list of some famous scientists from the EU and their discoveries.

Maths

Use tables or graphs to rank the EU nations by size, population and income. How do they compare when looked at in these different ways?

History

Look at how timelines help us to understand key moments in history. Use books and the Internet to research and create a timeline for the EU.

EU Countries

Geography

Describe the main geographical features of the EU as a whole. You might like to think about seas, mountains, rivers, forests and lakes.

Citizenship

The EU involves people from many different backgrounds working and living together. Think about the things that might be needed to help this to happen.

ICT

Use the Internet to try and find an audio clip of how to say 'hello' in different European languages. Practise saying 'hello' to each other and see how many of the EU languages you can collect.

English

Imagine that you have a pen pal in Turkey – one of the countries that wants to join the EU. What would you tell your friend about the EU? Why might people in Turkey want to join?

Further information and index

Further reading

Exploring Continents: Exploring Europe, Jane Bingham (Heinemann Library, 2007)
One Shot: The European Union Today, Simon Ponsford (Franklin Watts, 2007)
Regions of the World: Europe, Neil Morris (Heinemann Library, 2007)

Web

http://europa.eu/europago/welcome.jsp
An interactive page designed for younger learners to find out more about the EU nations and their history.
www.visiteurope.com/home.aspx
A tourism site for Europe, with very good information on each country and its cultural attractions.

Index